Airport Motel Redux:
A Suite For Bad Players

Poems by Mark Hennessy

Kansas City   Spartan Press   Missouri

Spartan Press
Kansas City, Missouri
spartanpresskc.com

Copyright (c) Mark Hennessy 2017
First Edition 1 3 5 7 9 10 8 6 4 2
ISBN: 978-1-946642-09-7
LCCN: 2017931389

Design, edits and layout: Jason Ryberg, Jeanette Powers
Cover design: j.d.tulloch
Author and cover photos: Trenton Lee Tiemeyer
All rights reserved. No part of this publication may be reproduced or transmitted in any form or by any means, electronic or mechanical, including photocopying, recording or by info retrieval system, without prior written permission from the author.

ACKNOWLEDGMENTS

Prospero's Books and Spartan Press would like to thank Jeanette Powers, j.d.tulloch, Jason Preu, M. Scott Douglass, Shawn Pavey, Shaun Savings, Jesse Kates, Jim Holroyd, Steven H.Bridgens, Thomas Mason, Beth Dille, Mason Wolf, Katherine Samet, The West Plaza Tomato Co., Mark Mclane, the Osage Arts Community and The Robert J. Deuser Foundation For Libertarian Studies.

Thanks to Jason *Baron Von Pork Pie* Ryberg, Will Leathem, Adam J Mason, my folks, Godzillionaire, steph and Kell, Dan Duncan

for Ezra

CONTENTS

The Airport Motel / 1
Parking for Customers Only! / 2
Parking Lot: Landscape by Parking Light / 4
Low Daily Rates! / 5
The Trojan Horse Room / 6
Yeah No: Body by Crazy / 7
Radio: godzillionaire: [Ex]communication / 8
Over the Honey Moon Is Over Room / 10
Guest Protocol: / 11
The Ruth Finlay Room / 12
Johnny Dollar Room / 13
The Room of Decaying Orbit / 14
The Case against de Academic Poet:
    How to annoy a poet be a poet / 15
Channel Zero: A[gal]matophilia / 18
Nature Channel: Den[drop]hilia / 19
Channel 13: Pygophilia / 20
Kansas History Channel: Mechanophilia / 21
Ghost Hunters: Spectrophilia / 22
History Channel: Narratophilia / 23
Lifetime Channel: Celebrophilia / 24
English Channel: Get it On Already / 25
Radio: 1950 DA: Child of God / 26
Sci-Fi Channel: *The Universe Contains*
  Wonders to Sate Appetites Both Refined and
  Gross But It Isn't for the Faint of Heart
  —Q to the Enterprise / 27

Game Show Channel: The Monty Hall Room / 28
The Bride of Frankenstein Room / 29
The Tiny Room of Gendered Expectations / 30
YOLO: The Room about the Traveling Salesman / 31
The Motel Juke: Lonely This Lonely That / 32
The Room of the Curator of Easy Fixes / 33
Keyless Entry: the Case against
       an Interventionist God / 34
We're Gonna Miss Us When We're Gone / 36
El Dopa Enlarges the Problem Semantic
   for Today's Gentleman / 37
Hotel Mail / Ghost Clone in Room Five-Oh: / 38
Great Ships Named for Women Going Down / 39
The Case of the Motel Architect:
    A Game of Sorrows / 40
Ask About Our Low Monthly Rate! / 41
Room 12: and Cried Last Before His Quiet / 42
It's Not About A Salary, It's All About Reality / 43
Pets Welcome / 44
El Dopa: Check This Guy Out / 45
Airport Motel Transliterated / 46
Just Between Us — I Want You & I to Have
   An Affair — On Us / 47
Collect Call from a Long Distance:
      Aeneas to Creüsa / 48

MONSIEUR M_____. JOURNAL ENTRY / 49
Epilogue: No.8. Psychic Clone. Taken From
        Voluntary Testimony Under Supervision Of
            The Investigatory Council.5.6.96. / 52
Room 9/11: the Case of   the Missing Pilot / 53
The Sad Affair of Room 19 Concluded:
    Cold Case Closed / 54
Efficiencies / 55
Nocturne in D / 56
You Did Me A Favor the Day You Left / 57
Good Wolf & Bad Wolf Have A
      Truth-Telling Contest / 58
Upon Request Bad Dog Sends a Selfie / 59
The Black Hole Room / 60

The happy ending is… a misrepresentation; for the world, as we know it, as we have seen it, yields but one ending: death, disintegration, dismemberment, and the crucifixion of our heart with the passing of the forms that we have loved.
 –Joseph Campbell

everything dies baby that's a fact/ maybe everything that dies some day comes back
 ~Bruce Springsteen

when you believe in things that you don't understand you suffer
 ~Stevie Wonder

that's when the beginning of the end begun
 ~Lana Del Rey

hanc ex diuerso sedem ueniemus in unam

delete delete delete delete delete delete delete delete
delete delete delete delete delete delete delete delete
delete delete delete delete delete delete delete delete
delete delete delete delete delete delete delete delete
delete delete delete delete delete delete delete delete
delete delete delete delete delete delete delete delete
delete delete delete delete delete delete delete delete
delete delete delete delete delete delete delete delete
delete delete delete delete delete delete delete delete
delete delete delete delete delete delete delete delete
delete delete delete delete delete delete delete delete
delete delete delete delete delete delete delete delete
delete delete delete delete delete delete delete delete
delete delete delete delete delete delete delete delete
delete delete delete delete delete delete delete delete
delete delete delete delete delete delete delete delete
delete delete delete delete delete delete delete delete
delete delete delete delete delete delete delete
delete delete delete delete delete delete delete delete
delete delete delete delete delete delete delete delete
delete delete delete delete delete delete delete delete
delete delete delete delete delete delete delete delete
delete delete delete delete delete delete delete delete
delete delete delete delete delete delete delete
delete delete delete delete delete delete delete delete
delete delete delete delete delete delete delete delete
delete delete delete delete delete delete delete delete
delete delete delete delete delete delete delete delete
delete delete delete delete delete delete delete delete

The Airport Motel

Welcome, he says.
He says I can see you're surprised the world didn't end.
He says I can see your surprise.
I can see you, he says.

Are you alone, he says.
He says or are you w/ someone,
he says the rates change
depending on, he says

Do you not want to play anymore, he says.
He says, if you want to play do you want
or do you not want to be it, he says.
Staying long, he says.

He says like planes answer plans,
He says, comfortable room, free air, ice machine.
Check out time he says —
He says, check out time

Parking for Customers Only!

She looks like she
                always is waiting for some
one to ask her if
                she wants anything —
She looks like so
                there is always waiting some
one near to ask her
                if she wants anything —
She says no like she
                cannot come out on the porch
                for 1 second
She says no like she
                has company she says no
                like do not cry
She says no like she
                will hose down the chair we are in
She says no like she
                will call our sister, no like call the cops
She says no like we
                know how to get a girl
                but not how to keep one
She says no like we
                live in a fairy-tale about
                astronauts & boobs

She says no like
                the next guy will be tall
                & like us not at all
She says no like
                a bigger dick w/ better teeth
                & minus the art
She says no like she
                is not wearing her ring in her heart
She says no like she
                told us she did not want to get married

She leaves us her smell
                her hair on our pillowcase —
She leaves us her hair
                in the drain. We mean she leaves us.

Parking Lot: Landscape by Parking Light

We think that our hymns of praise, we
think our hymns of sorrow, are hymns
of sense—but all sense dissipates w/
our singing back to the sole hymn of sil
ence. There, that's better. Now wait.

Our house is as full of the ghosts
that will be as the ones that were.
Which is to write empty.
Somewhen our entangled twin
lies weeping on a farmhouse floor
while his wife hustles kids into our car.

His excited state is the briefest fluctuation
before the needle returns where it double
-ought. All that stuff flying around outside
is illiterate—the word inside our bubble,
the waving siren of our world, the side
yard full of alphabet-shaped specters,

shades we know we're this close away
from seeing & best, ignorant of. The
door opens & a small yellow light blooms
at our knee above the emergency brake
& these things are organized out from
the confusion for us: the tattered fringe
of our jeans, our boots, the gas pedal, floor
board & where we're sitting that's all to see.

Low Daily Rates!

do you take this man takes another
do you take another
                                      man
                                      woman
do you take another
do you take this woman takes another

for better or worse gets worse for rich
for rich or poor gets poor for
                                      sick
                                      health
poor for good & bad times
good times & bad times to hold lets go

what roa(go)d joins air port
separates
                                      obey
                                      depart
go from this day forward —
go

The Trojan Horse Room

For a moment our house of cards held
& seemed a grand dreaming & ridiculous,
a place to live in from the outside, happy
even, even when the susceptibility of its

support made collapse understood at the
time of construction. What we mean to write
is how it, light, looks like one thing & be
haves like another. What we think gift

we hold close until its veiled fire undoes all
w/out — take up our photo albums? Our power's
down, we have none. Presented two things:
your gift & absence, we took both w/o question,

like a cartoon rabbit handed us a bomb & we,
too confused to do more than hold it tight, we
aring the face we all do when we are somewhere
else, inside, trying to get the joke.

Yeah No: Body by Crazy

Room 11 is Body by Meth & Dirt Bike
Room 12 is Body by Lucky Strike
Room 13 is Body by Vanity
Room 14 is Body by Rum & Coke

The Front Desk Clerk is Body by Sixty-Two

Room 15 is Body by Accident
Room 16 is Body by Empty
Room 17 is Body by the Road
Room 18 is Body by Body by Body

Room 19 is Body by Baby by Baby
Room 20 is Body by Books
Room 21 is Body by Burning
Room 22 is Us Trying to Hold onto the Ghost of

You

Radio: godzillionaire: [Ex]communication

Divorce was her idea
but I got a reputation
for every little thing
for wrestling every
kind of bear, meanest
one to fight's honey
listen closer now
I say a truth you
need to hear
all this reaching out
hysteria is drawing near

I don't wanna say right
don't wanna say wrong
I just wanna say done
just wanna say gone

you know how it is at the end —
you start to consider the beginning
all those faces are chains
tryin' to reel you in
lover in your eye
keeps pulling me
back to place —
this was a favorite once,
now I can't quite
place the face —

donna wanna say right
don't wanna say wrong
just wanna say done
just wanna say gone
gone daddy gone

Over the Honey Moon Is Over Room

Pick from any of these twelve shabby rooms —
all that is required is that we be alone together.
We thought the beginning too full to deplete —
there will be no peace in this parting, choose.

Here is the place where you can be a man &
I can be a woman alone together in our rented
bed of history's mistakes. What relief to try
each other on only if to want ourselves anew.

We mean we still name our dog, dead a decade,
everyday — how could our goodbye not crush us
past caring? We mean, our blood kin are throwin
g our children from the tall places so we all bear

witness: we can say yes or we can say no & no
thing changes w/ the saying but us. Now
get in the room & draw the shitty shades shut.
Agree to come together to/in this place before.

Guest Protocol:

Rule 11: The Guest Must Ask the Fortune-Teller
Rule 12: The Fortune-Teller Must Give Bad News
Rule 13: Actions Taken to Circumscribe Must Ensure Consequence

Rule 14: No Approaching the Windows After Occupancy
Rule 15: Shut the Fuck Up
Rule 16: Your Silence May Save You Your Life

Rule 17: For a Time the Time Must Be Sweet
Rule 18: This Sweet Time Must Be Short
Rule 19: This Sweet Time Must In Time Be Forgot

Rule 20: There Must Come a Child
Rule 21: The Child Must Be a Singer
Rule 22: The Singer Must Sing This Song

this song must be sweet
this song must be short
this song must be forgot

The Ruth Finlay Room

The airport motel maid blues sings in each motel guest
who seeks her—the woman of the house in each motel
guest has a mind like each motel room: the strangeness
of each particular diminishes against the rest: she's ring

ing the desk/she's throwing things into her bag, she's gr
abbing the tiny soap—knock yourself out the maid says
— the woman on the phone has a voice like a motel room
— says Where is your wife? Where is it safe? like a chain/s

   Now to get the beds made before the place burns down.

he holds up the woman in her voice has words like a cha
in/drags to hold it up or care to hear each black word a li
nk that makes the chain of our talk heavier—the woman in
the motel room has a body like a house she's building ju

st so she can chain a dog to it, a voice like a chain that sp
eaks only to finger the links/while she thinks about nobod
y she's burning a cake a chain like a clock like a link like
a tick off a letter bomb. Self-Destructive? We All Say *Yes.*

Johnny Dollar Room

On our drive in our car our kids anti
cipate our room: push-pin pillows, steel
-wool blankets — & no hospital nowhere

close delivers. One more road side white
cross & we got travel BINGO. It's pretty
American to couch everything as a problem.

The problem for our divorce investigator is,
well, we'd tell but you'd guess in the time it
took us to — you bring that shit home w/

you: we notice when you take the phone
into any room other than the one we are
all in, when all your interactions beg some

delete: penny-ante head games w/ life
or death pay-outs. Oh, the debt! we sing
the debt! The debt blackens the sky & all

we sing besides is where the fuck were you?

The Room of Decaying Orbit

When we remember later those details that stuck out like
a turd in a punchbowl then — the strangers en-scéne all re-
semble actors playing undercover narcs — too hopped on
their own bullshit to smell ours — the guy who's swinging

his shirt over his head in a circle while we wait for the mail
truck, the guy who shoulders in next to us at the bar & his
narcy smile, his narcy watch, his whole narcy vibe, man.
We lived in red-flag city then, had close-readers, but they

were cops, man, knocking on our friend's doors, because
we sent our selves packages there, because in our business
it pays not to advertise, because of chronic pain in our
membrane, because we are not gonna tote that bail on

instructional pay, dig. So we never call the cruise line back
to confirm, we won already by not writing this in jail — &
plenny plenny we could 've, shot at & nullified previous,
trying to get outta town before someone other than our ex

puts us all down.

The Case against de Academic Poet:
How to annoy a poet be a poet

& you know it, you come to in de hall(no)way of yer
too-mediocre-to-be-the-force-for-evil-to which-they-
aspire nemesis: anemic, +or- gives you apathanesia —
                              uh, where were you? —
outside his study door is, ah, armor suit, mit visor,
halberd, mace, the whole bit & then when you take it all
in, a dumbwaiter opens at hall's end on the wall
above walnut wainscoting & you try to recall where in
the house you are & did this tiny elevator come up
or come down
alligator?   there's a prophet's head on a silver
salver inside, Clyde — [sings down down, doobie
do-do-do-do-doobie] — that sound drifts down,
down the shaft — out onto yer yard pard, makes y'all
Ethel Merman fembots in the kiddy pool full of hose-water
& cans of Hamm's squeal, rub themselves hard into g-
strings & X-plode wit' pleasure punk!
A party forms like cotton candy randy — a hopped-up low-
rider
  pulls up/   /shudders to the concrete
        where Tee-Pees Café regular laters curbed
the poet's big smart fat fucking mouth like cotton
candy & glows — the Riviera's gorgeous lilac-color
ground effect — the door [Public Enemy] opens —
Chuck D.'s basso spills out — fills de air your head
is in — a party like cotton candy couple of big fine

bitches step out/   / drinking Cristal from the bottle
& hike up they skirts both & piss & laugh w/ the pleasure
punk — mister driver leans over the stick to address you
through air above the Buick's pass[death]enger seat, his
ate-up eight-ball eyes spinning w/ all the Adderall he
[medicine] on — & he hard to hear over the Public

Enemy — but it sound like he bitching 'bout the weight
& & laughing at you[me] — down, down, doobie, do do
— & telling us get in

Pay Channels

Channel Zero: A[gal]matophilia

Oh! strollaround-wavy eastsidewalks of LFK,
you were our good playground, but too short-lived
— the good times, in everydream home on our route

a heart moves an empty couch out to the yard to make
room for the new ache that's coming: shitty sums it
upright? to love some one who can not love us back?

That toe-sucking pygmielion had one thing right, tho,
weird-scienceing his dreamgal thru chiselstrike: we find
the beauty we look for, & while our love's not about it,

everything else is, dollface, the radiosong, the alleyshadow
we cast w/o Sheryl, the empty space inside us, the smile
we try to keep, our try to walk our away back to a place

where she is waiting for us, hasn't left, or been stolen,
look, there! past the gates! she hasn't moved an inch.

Nature Channel: Den[drop]hilia

Yes! Missum, we do hit trees harder than son bono —
Que? Chere? Don't say oh no! worse ways we know
there are to go by far: paperclip, paperclip, grinder

man, blow: green bowl half moon so half wolf, half
high, like us, gus, man is that us far out below the burn
line, & prophets get stoned by sinners high as kites

doin' the velvet rut shuffle: stoned like lava & low
like planes puff/puff/pass solving for air castles sit
ting on our ass. On the bus. Dude. Don't we just love

it when someone tells us what God loves & does not
love for us to love: the things of this world or of any
other, where every green thing afire smokes itself

to death, no air no breath, no piece no peace: a rocket
race, running on sour diesel, caught up in tall branches.

Channel 13: Pygophilia

The invitation arrives! A Telegram! Invited
to dinner by our self-declared cannibal King,
Georgia weighs her options: to eat or be eat

en — Georgia, baby, if you decide to go, do
your best not to look too delicious — don't act
like you don't know what we mean — you're in

danger baby. He'll get suspicious if you walk all
side-ways. He is a professional. Paid to eat: a
dream. You must, in such company, do your level

best to hide that beautiful butt. It looks so damn
nutritious awful things could happen — My God!
A diner, unfamiliar w/ social codes that forbid that

food, might be pardoned to start there — might be
understood. Lord knows I would, with all my heart.

Kansas History Channel: Mechanophilia

Miss Amelia, where are you now? In a flight-path
meadowlark halo? Angel you built like a rocket ship,
streamlined & occupationally as likely to explode, oh,

as crash, as drown, in love with the throttle &
the stick, the lift & dark vector of our blind maw driving
us. Strung out like a 2,558 mile-long string of pearls across

the zero floor of night ocean — flying somewhere between
our moon & Howland island — who among us would
electralove the Lockheed's buckety nuts & bolts? Who

would grinddown into the cockpit tighter? Into a span
of joy? Any one of us who found ourselves there: neither
the machine nor her lover knowing if the other capable

of what is asked: to stay in the air longer. Meely got a plane
stuck in her heart at the age of ten, never got it out again.

Ghost Hunters: Spectrophilia

See! A trace of old streetcar-track under our East Lawrence brick, & inside on the wall there, an empty land line jack, under paler squares where our portraits used to hang &

outside a door bell & a coal bin chute, a pylon hook under our Kaw bridge just for Sour Pete, the Colonel pacing in 506, still strange fruit up in the big Sigma house from

Lorraine & Ed, & Leroy Harris sets his cigar down & downtown buildings burn again; cuz the truth is we all in love with ghosts — don't wanna love change when it's the

only choice, don't wanna love no body but the dead — the lovers of our youth loiter moon-faced outside our bed chambers where we all best judge the appetites of the living

[   ] think! I woke late with my dead dog on my chest, collapsed my arms around her until I hugged myself for the loss of true love, played nevermind til I remembered

all the snow we dance in began as streams of tears.

History Channel: Narratophilia

After the funeral, of course, or before, depending on what
you came here for, is a must of lust, & in our church base
ment, & our bedrooms, & the back-seats of our cars, & in

the beds of trucks, flatbeds & flowerbeds, & featherbeds, &
waterbeds, & roadbeds, & restaurant bathrooms & after
-hour bars, & back-seats, repeats, & in train parks, & spas,

in swim-club showers, & in trap-house hours & in drive-in
lots, his places, her places, & in no-tell motels, in hotels, & in
holiday inns, & road-side gin-dives, & beach-side rentals, in

PKP/WCs, & in our mirrors, & reflections of our glass, &
off wood path & lakebed & riverbed & park gazebo, in west
stacks, & on car hoods, & in the car wash, Tunnel of Love,

on our honeymoons at Niagara Falls, in upholstered chairs
& yoga balls, quiet at the in-laws, stifling cries on the stairs.

Lifetime Channel: Celebrophilia

On the reality runway show the beautiful German
bird of prey challenges her groundlings to execute
a design that says America. Since we like to play a

long at work we gather materials: yards of investment
bankers buying life-insurance policies from positive
bleeders, a sixteen-year-old bolt in a sixty-thou$and

car texting where are you muddled in her accidental
vehicular manslaughter, a foot of crush videos, skeins
of smoking rubble unrolling over all the landscape.

Night-light pollution creates an opportunity to rename
old constellations: the Colon, the Boob & Navel, the other
star, the Reverse Period. A million books written an hour

in six seconds or less — nobody reading nothing. If all
the adults were making love the children could play any
where. We pretend to honor life but the family of mice

our waste feeds reunites in the trashcan, goodbyes muff-
ling in the tan plastic shopping bag — the flag of our cap
ricious nation —waving to one another through the traps

they carry inside themselves. When we burn those pages
of books we can remember burn also, like an ex's kiss.
We are all fractals of decreasing magnitude. You like this.

English Channel: Get it On Already

Lover, come here for a second &
look at my hunger —

spread the fat across the sheets,
or desk, or coats behind you in the closet,

our fingers,
our mouths,

anchor this moment in
salt & musk for us

to remember when we are alone,
the buttons now, the ribbon, I need

your swollen pulse on my tongue,
the torture of the tease is sweetest

in its final reel,
our hands inside,

mouths open,
lover hurry,

hurry,
please.

Radio: 1950 DA: Child of God

I took her body
back to Cold Mountain
threw her clothes down the well

now when I water
I can remember
I know I going to hell

what does it matter?
nothing's nothing,
I'm a child of god motherfucker
poor little lonesome me

if you come looking
for different answers
you come ready for war

youre gonna find out
just like your brother
who had to find out for sure

what does it matter?
nothing's nothing,
I'm a child of god motherfucker
poor little lonesome me

Sci-Fi Channel: *The Universe Contains
Wonders to Sate Appetites Both Refined and
Gross But It Isn't for the Faint of Heart*
—Q to the Enterprise

When you first hear a deaf parent wish
for a deaf child it doesn't make sense. But
then you are not deaf. Systems are organized
by the faith and science of belief. The first
time you hear a teacher argue to the Kansas
Board of Education that the Earth is six
thousand years old it doesn't make sense,
but then you see the one idiot embraced
by his fellow idiots and what could you say
to keep a kid out of the Crips that doesn't
apply to this guy? The cosmos is dying
for lack of heat we create in surplus. Cause
in cosmology— the problem simply put is
that everything accelerates away from
everything   else
without any observable cause: galaxies
rushing toward unknown visual properties
of possibility, an asymmetry that exits as
oblivion, wanting to be somewhere further,
rushing towards the boundless like lovers
at the airport. I should write your oblivion is
symmetric because it is truer. Your identity is
based in division/   violence,
your micro articulates in all exact ways the macro,
you spinning reaching hungry thing.

Game Show Channel: The Monty Hall Room

Dear little birdy, what we writing is me what we meaning is you will we want to trade our prize fo r what's behind door 22? we expect that we do — we owe curiosity's due — to wear where it will & th en send us the bill — even w/ all our family in the studio audience crying no! crying boo hoo till the ir tops are wet — crying don't' forget! Crying righ t to left, from aft to zef, crying, pleas: Another da y! Another Dollar! You wear our ring like a colla r! Birdy, Please! Don't forget birdy what you san g when you left, you sang: more players want to play than will be allowed to play, & our proble m posed this way presents a solution both ludicro us & demonstrably true about how things are w/ m e & you: prisoners or traders both, either, eh birdie ? Fuck that shit hombre — little birdies all must choo se. Then all little birdies can trade what we got wh ich will require only that we let go go of what we grasp tight so tightly so-so. Tell us what sport? Tha t cross-addiction can come on down? Who here in our audience can show me: pornography-free histo ry? trash bag empty of recyclables? Cruelty-free l anguage? Vanity-free poetry? Your all's yaller dog is top bitch till you see Miss Daisy — & the blue me rle coat on that 'un ah hers got us wonderin' about door three — looks so good stretched out alone on t he clean sheet all by itself don't it?:

word

The Bride of Frankenstein Room

The ghost of our humanity has followed us to the end
of our Earth, & she looks like our wife. Being born be
autiful has taught her one lesson; becoming poor, anot
her — & tho we stitch together an amalgam, monster is
what we make, everytime. So, come let's scour the tab
le w/ our tears & elbow grease: our maker wants thin

gs clean when he returns, & our hair combed, & our m
oney wisely invested, & our places prepared for his arr
ival: lover put down your torch & pitchfork, do — nothi
ng has changed in the story since its first telling — we'd
think we'd fight harder to accept but it's so much easyie
r to blame our shamblequilt groping child — bad, bad, ba

d ismantled by the architect before completion or use
out of spite for the room next door — every motel has 1
love story it keeps for itself as a myth about itself — 1
story moaning & crying on the floor before the door,
DO NOT RESUSSITATE tattooed across a breast lit
from w/in by a bleating neon heart — it's never a house

one of us in the crowd asks if there's a doctor in, shabo
om, shaboom, we wonder at the ascension of our crude
materials: from the nether to the paper & uploaded back
into the nether again in a multitude of forms shimmering,
Oh!, we tangoed 'til we were good & sore Aladdin, a lad, &
a lass, just trying to piece it to get her — Oh!, tenderness
you were our harshest mistress yet.

The Tiny Room of Gendered Expectations

Mimi Smith's *Steel Wool Peignoir* —
stuck in a box on campus talking to poets
about form. Part of it's really soft, we see
through it, a thrill — remember other night

(   )
gowns as fine if not fuller & we stretch
a hand out unthinking to touch, what? before
it bumps a gainst this invisible barrier so

we are just left looking — let a look caress,
what, are those S.O.S pads? Hard to tell
from out here. All we can do is imagine
how rough — uncomfortable it must be to

actually have near you in bed — how much
it would hurt to put on, how impossible,
once in, to embrace any one, how it's best,
only,   worn inside the eye.

YOLO: The Room about the Traveling Salesman

Yo Holmes — Seeya! Hope you live 'til you
don't mi hermosas, mi paragiiauptirimicawios!
Retrosynthetic Love Rules — X-President Ge
orge W. Bush Drools! Skeeb now? Bet. iGre
en: When I bid you good luck I mean with yer he
aducation not yer education — a more pressing
current existential pot(to spud or not to spud)ato
for you than the Rock-N-Roll finish:

            but I go on 'bout whiskey
& death so you must think me grumpy — No
way, José. I am the aforementioned guitar
albeit high-tuned, not for adolescent bell
igerents — but for music, baby! Kachaaws!

           try life five miles straight sky-up —
but that's my life that's how it's cut:
but you and I drink now different cups
gots titillated suds you gots ketchup

Still glad we met, are not I? The truths we
shared better than drug therapy. Radical.
But not better than hugs Fletcher? Is not
knowing [kisses > wisdom] a wisdom?
Damarcus, will you remember ferruginosa
means rust-colored? Jake — what does the ghost

of Keats whisper to you now? Cough-cough.
'ere — Steph is this a send-off?

The Motel Juke: Lonely This Lonely That

Always sounds good in Honky-Tonk, this
constant fleeing from ear bit gig to shitty gig,
singing the world's saddest song, but exhausted
& well-lit is how we feel. But it's habit not choice
now, not just that we don't wanna punch a clock —
buying debt in whatever absurdi$t   compromi$e
brings us to sell our day to another — we tried — we k
ept finding ourselves in some school's battleship grey
cinder block stairwell crying & asking ourselves Why?
Heartbroke's why & we're sorry to sing it so
true — but that's how this song goes about us &
you — us drinking ourselves to death in a bar w/
the boys asking why you won't let yourself love
us no more — besides obvious you don't want
to — So. Here's some stuff we quit
from Hard to Hardest to do:
Shooting Smack
Smoking Cigarettes
Thinking about You

The Room of the Curator of Easy Fixes

He acts like we've just met, this guy —
like our name is a foot locker he's trying
to haul up the basement steps w/ regrets
like our conversation is a heavy chain:
him w/ the running end — us the anchor
asking him how he's been, he's been

      staring over our left shoulder's what.
He acts like what he's thinking about
is a big deal, like he's better than bills

in the mail, better than a TV binge, chills
outside town, acts like Tchaikowski is cool,
like Idol isn't, like he isn't hungry, like

he doesn't need to look at his phone, him.
He looks dirty, drunk, stinky, stoned, pre
occupado, like he should but won't look

guilty, exhausted, wind-bedraggled, like
his outfit was pulled behind a truck thru
a tire dump & shot at, like a health-risk

at a public pool, like an invitation to be strip
-searched at the border, like swap seats
in an airplane seat, like an away from every
one else at a motel, like a dog, a fluke,
a john, a mark, a door mat, not like
a zero but like a double zer00

Keyless Entry: the Case against
an Interventionist God

i.

the woman on the phone has a voice like a motel
room she's throwing things into her bag grabbing
the lousy soap yes pillowcases it yes you see in her

preparations a case being made against us, against
our body, the woman in the motel room has a voice
like a house she's selling: kid stuff in boxes, our stu

ff in trash bags — the cases we two get down to will
punish us candy-like, now & later, not for our anger
but w/ our anger — like grendel-monster outside y

our private window looking in, teethgnashing — ho
w long are you going to last? we ask the hangover,
the 20, parked in our car at the edge of the lot not t

o stop the car but to stop this old family business f
rom eating us up from laughing at us & let me tell
you laughing at us, at the petty inviolable madness

of the concerns of our hour, our infinitesimally pet
ty thing. So when the woman on the phone tells us
she doesn't love us it felt like her kiss to another

leaning together pretty in her car—looking back
the only view of her wanting to kiss afforded us

ii.

please lord, give us shelter in this our lot, this host
ile territory—please lord, save us before we suicide
by cop by smack by car by jingo by choking by birth

by rope by dope by smoke by cleaning up by fire by
dad's gun by pillowcase & pond by shovel by bomb
by plan by plane by brother by each other protect us

from those who suicide from highway & airport, fro
m the sums of autism, from the subtraction of birth,
from the enemy inside our gates, from AIDS, earthquakes

& tea-party republicans, from snakes in the
donkey's straw, from reading her diary, from landfill
overflow, from conceptual artists, from art. Save us from

hearing her say you better want to know what you want
to know before we arrive to where we have been driving
all along—love unhinges this door—turns its force

inwards as storms named for women violenter
toward the eye do. Ok. Say come on. Say we must
not be denied. The door gives a little to the chain &

the heat & the cold exchange in words we will not
write. Nor forget. We offered a dog to the door &
a child to the latch.

              & the door gave way

                                to the latch & the latch

gave way

We're Gonna Miss Us When We're Gone

& when for long no one has touched us for a
time our jamming ourselves into a small tub
is apostrophe to sex as is our fist-fight, our rock

song, our inebriation, as our sex is apostrophe to
god, as god is apostrophe to god — we are alone
in a room remembering the home bed in the motel

tub that any bed is apostrophe to the home bed
the home is apostrophe to the family, the family
is apostrophe to its members, its members apostrophe

to that word, the word apostrophe to the thing itself —
remembering your words this word is missing
your hand on our body like the meniscus of tub

water drawn lightly down our body as the tub
drains, down the crooks of our arms, tickle down
our haunches in the motel tub, down past the small of

our back, down through the under-cathedral of our toes,
away from our asking again w/ each breath the drain
takes the water that rushes away from us down

the motel drain to come back please, please,
please baby come back please come back please —

El-Dopa Enlarges the Problem Semantic for Today's Gentleman

What we said was welcome
What we meant was let's go

What we said was I wonder who it is
What we meant was lucky they don't know

What we said was never again
What we meant was we already forgot

What we said was no way, not again
What we meant was rolled up in our sock

What we said was seems nice
What we meant was hope he chokes

What we said was we'll check
What we meant was no way

What we said was thanks for sound advice
What we meant was get bent

What we said was mortgage
What we meant was rent

What we said was sorry —
What we meant was let's fuck

What we said was congratulations
What we meant was good luck

Hotel Mail / Ghost Clone in Room Five-Oh:

Dear Ramon, do you ever have those moments upon
waking where your disorientation is of such a nature, as is
the dream you have just been dreaming & awoken from,

as is your lifestyle, that to determine whether you are
awake or dreaming is an effort of time & of con sideration?
have you had this on the floorboard of a van to open the

cargo door & stand reeling in our motel parking lot?
a place marked by near light of sunrise or twilight,
& in the air & activity about you no clue as to which?

We check our bodies, our pockets for clues & get dis
turbing evidence? Where did that come from did we
ask ourselves? & again of our expanding bruise—do

you get behind motel door & feel as tho this place were
yours? do you draw the latch & bolt & call this, for now,
safety, when even less at risk isn't right? do you draw

the blinds & say unseen but your copy in the mirror stares
& starts at the least noise?—why would any of us petition
to keep him amongst us?   silly!

Great Ships Named for Women Going Down

Titania? She's reclined to grant or deny access — Oh
holy succubus, oh well-shaped heel, oh either side the veil
birth parts — please, please, don't talk us to death tonight.
But she, mad prioress, demands respect only true love
might prove, small-hour bell-rings demand polish: an entry
wound here, exit there, claw-marks on the roofs of
wardrobes under scoring her approbation, divots, tracks
left in wisteria patch when she reversed her armored car
backing over Lucky, her shout: *Au revoir,* the sin or corpse
rolled-up cargo: a stained carpet, a memento dumpster-
headed. Ah, stolen moments, ah, midnight salon, ah, pretend
surprise, ah, you in your bedclothes tiger. Ah how soft the soft
parts look! But turns she her deaf ear to all our baby babys,
our beg: background radiation: the cicadas in the trees.
She says: the Dodge, the delays, these days, but means you,
or me, or demands, or appetite only distance understands, or
such remove, or interruption by authorities, or nosey
neighbors, or jealous Panda Garden deliveryman blushing in
what's left of us, our garden, or the North Atlantic, or what's
left of icebergs there, or ice, skyscraper-sized, or Saturn, or its
ring, or bodies far from one an other, or the song they sing —
come closer, comecloser,
or every body walking around like everything is all infinite &
shit, or how every particulate we know isn't, or guess, or grab,
or our bed raggled playmate, or the scruff of her neck, or her
ball gown in the dryer, or her hot cup of ginger tea, or us on
both knees, appropriate, or her bandage, or her stellar history,
or her destiny common to us all.

The Case of the Motel Architect:
A Game of Sorrows

Dog's drunk enough to draw against Bear & dumb
enough to do it: Grins, tongue lolls house left & flips
The-Sorrow-of-Lee-When-He-Left-A-Testicle-Atop-
The-Chain-Link-Fence-Behind-The-Liquor-Store-A-

Lifelong-Sorrow-He-Bore-Alone-Until-He-Married.
Bear plays The-Sorrow-of-the-Single-Mother-at-the-
Grocery-Store-Putting-Items-Back. Dog turns over
The-Sorrow-of-Widower-Reading-Wife's-Texts. A

push. Bear cuts into a 12-month spread w/ his minus-1
paw—The-Sorrow-of-Miners-w/-Pregnant-Wives.
Everybody bets. & what's at hazard is always the same.
Around their game patrons stop & wait for the pressure

to let off. The-Sorrow-of-the-Teenage-Queer-in-Love-w/-
the-Quarterback. A push or Dog's down. Bear plays
The-Sorrow-of-the-Slaughterhouse-Janitor. Dog comes
back w/ The-Sorrow-of-the-Family-Court-Judge.
Now Dog's all in. The Sorrow-of-Finite-Cups-of-Coffee.

Bear's up & trying to close: The-Sorrow-of-the-Mother-
Reading-the-Friendly-Fire-Telegram. Dog, irritated:
The-Sorrow-of-the-Parent-Who-Buries-Their-Child.
Bear angry enough to turn: The-Sorrow-of-
the-Nation-that-Buries-Their-Children

Ask About Our Low Monthly Rate!

Three sirens sing there at runway's end, song
-words that fall like rain water against parched
lips, beauty singers eye-aching, dark halos of

kinky hair, wet sparkly dresses — better hurry —
This landing strip concrete is broadwater say,
Cessnas, ships, wind in the brome blows forward,

tilts wheat-white into itself at the top, reaching
inside to divide & break, to stack itself in white
noise against the broken mouth-rock of the levee —

why don't you hurry, come on boy, see about me?
How they sway? W/ palms open & down, bodies
trap for deaf bodies. Travelers unbroken by their song

they are none & we driven by wind for so long that in
their song, our rushing towards now we are driven to
& not by it. Three sirens sing — the petrichor swells —

blue spangles/low-cut dress — Our pilot's name will
come, after this, to mean, long journey-not mistake —
but trying to make it to a home no longer there is

righter.

Room 12: and Cried Last Before His Quiet

The clown in 22 cried all day yesterday
And all night last night
What words did he say while crying?
Just one. Just the one name.

It's Not About A Salary, It's All About Reality

the clown comes out eleven is a buck
buck fifty & all man

                                         retina

spins like ah man
shouts where de maid where de shit

nooner the gardener plows profs gal
begin break

                                         lunch

end break
until dey both ready fer dudder tago

the runt run off the levee is a runner
stone to stone

                                         stoned

& line to end
of the line where line run stone end:

Pets Welcome

So all the Janes Doe we know know her, the vampire,
in classroom, book, on screen — study her pretty little
cruelties, expressions, in play, in bed, *en el Cuidad del
Fantasmas*, in heat, in town, at night in our head. So
all the Janes Doe we know try her on for size, play her
how? in our scene — to seduce or destroy? Dance a tight
-wire between go away, come close.   Go away.
So all the Janes Doe we know get good at quiet when
we ask, get good at gasoline smile when we cry water,
get good at being seen laughing in cars on dates jes when
we come outta market wit' Kleenex & ice-cream, man we
so sad sack it's a scream, get game the worse we get at play,
get good to play while we work, get good at work when we
ask to play, get a better look the worse we stare, get good at
forgot to call the worse we hope to hear, get good at phone
talk when we in the same room, keeps our letters unopened
in a stack we can see pacing her block Jimmie Mack &
never calls never kisses back, Jack — Jane gets good going
out for worse we get at waiting, gets better at ignore the
more we pretty please, gets good at forgetting to wear her
ring, blushing, laughing, sucking face while we get
crowned the jerk-off king.

El Dopa: Check This Guy Out

caught you gardening in the air before
the motel door, oh, you found a flower

amidst the weeds — marvel at its heady breath
make mouths at children in your class

put together little letters after
your name — a silly game & you knew

like school was a room
you could put your poem in

going in: tell the truth & lose
or lie & win —

so you say back I do
to what you're supposed to —

& underneath ever word you say is another
word that means, however spelled, defiance

& at last you knew poetry as artifice.
Absolute only in silence.

Airport Motel Transliterated

E ach of my rooms has been many rooms to man y
p eople. Too many people. & each asked us ov e
r to be new daily. We wonder if, after a long time o
f not missing, if a time is coming where we will mis

s you. Your heat & noise locked into place, a sens e
d eep in my material that your living all over me wa
s an inevitability. The airport believes it made hu m
a ns happy because so many rushed & clang towa r

d s each other inside & for a while I felt the same u
n til I came to know the violence inherent in you r
n earness. Then it seemed that those of you who s
t ayed alone made happiest sense, rested, & did n

ot labor against an other. But, erect too long besi d
e the airport, the road, I know no value in rest be s
i de suspicion & worry: wake up, I want to shake y
o u from my bed, wake up, it is time for you to g o.

Just Between Us — I Want You & I to Have An Affair — On Us

God did us both a favor when god gave you that ass —
is every smallest thing impalable? We are talking to
that part of you that would rather finish washing dishes

than make-out on the couch. Ouch. The onions heart
we thought too sharp until we tried it in our dish &
learned a right. We thought wives read their husband's

verse until we married. We thought marriage love's
union until we learned from our bills to be solemn
about our debts. Until we learned from our home

comings to take our time returning. Until our future
learned from our past we had no lover else. We thought
we had so much to say at our parting, until we learned

from our parting
that only the silence between us says it all.

Collect Call from a Long Distance:
Aeneas to Creüsa

The sound file opens. White noise breaks over the
telephone line. He may as well be calling from a prison
ship. She may well as be dead. We listen as the distance

between them in creases, leaping miles in those pauses
where, after she says she will accept charges, he tries to
gather words that signify more than the impossibility of

their reunion swelling between them/ & so an other
second passes, & another, until it can no longer support
the connection & lets go & on his end those words he

fought so to assemble slipped from his side of the knot &
tumbled back into the abyss in which their utterance had
been, in its inception, preconfigured, destined, & in

which their lack of reception certain. When we tried to
conceive what he might say to her No! & Please! & Don't
Go! was all we could invent but far off since between his

throat closing w/ mere grief or on the brine of his tears
what he said was this: just small pathetic noises w/out
purchase on the things he'd set to bind them to

MONSIEUR M_____. JOURNAL ENTRY

Small dual-prop airplane leaving Kansas now famous for happiness. New mountain range, new river, new excellent sparkling paint on arrival walkway. Say, for the sake of argument, that I don't make it to Krakow in time, that like a lot of other people who aren't expecting this to be their last day it is and I don't make it. While we've got some time to kill here en route allow me to recite my accomplishments in the Othelloic hope you may love me more to hear them: I owned a Buick. I ate a plate of jalapeños. I survived a murderous attempt on my life by someone who, as Madame Zora correctly predicted in a ceremony that involved loose-leaf tea of a particularly fragrant variety, "was well known to me," I circumnavigated the globe, I performed daily ritualistic musical procedures calculated to best reveal the depth and intensity of my satisfaction, and I lived like a cowboy lightening-quick-draw villain, without responsibility or expectation, in a motion that was a constant and perfect tour of everything the world has to offer, staying in any one place only a little longer than the amount of time required to leave it, which underlined the temporal nature of everything, making everything more or less okay, and beautiful even but sad, myself weaving, 5-O'Clock in the morning drunk, almost hands and knees drunk, in the long line to check in for my flight back to wherever whatever exit I had last taken to moon over some new girl had arbitrarily made my home, my books the only thing I carried with me, dictionary and bible and Whitman, the only objects I insisted on having near me and the airport thronging with people all of whom made couples composed of mama and toddler, until I got so hot and dizzy with all the left-over hurt that I got sick, and since I was out in public, in the airport full of mothers who were regarding me with forthright concern, I only had my bag but it contained books, so I threw up into the large pocket of my greatcoat at the same time that the giant purple dinosaur showed up at the gate and all the children cheered and screamed and I had the confused notion that the kids were responding collectively, sarcastically, to my embarrassing emesis. At the height of my power, I owned the best gentleman's gentleman then on the market. I read a lot. I drank a lot. I was a thoughtful and grateful citizen of the planet. I was in love with all its manifestations. I loved its crawling and beautiful animals, its deserts, the radiant all-night heat of the metropolis. I got scared sometimes, like I am now. When I get frightened by something, by my consideration of some act, I let myself be afraid but I breathe and do it, the thing, like with the train, like with the wave in New Zealand I told you about. Sometimes it was just being alone that was most frightening for me but when I breathed into it, then I drank wine and played the Polonaises of Chopin and read The Man with The Blue Guitar aloud to the dog, then the fear became a gift. He could see the sky behind the stewardess, with the sunshine refracting from the cloud surface in a shade of Klimt's gold, the sky-blue of her uniform, he was reminded of the Madonna. He had been inside his writing. He was disoriented. Distracted by the good smell of her coffee and the nice scratchy noise her hose made as she shifted her stance and spoke again.

Czy mogę pomóc?
Dziekuje.
Gotta go. We're preparing the cabin for arrival.

Epilogue: No.8. Psychic Clone. Taken From Voluntary Testimony Under Supervision Of The Investigatory Council.5.6.96.

When I awoke it was like I had come out of a fever. Like I had been in bed while it was nice outside. And then wanted the more to be out in the sun. Funny now, right? I made really strong coffee and the coffee was good. I poured it over ice. I shook the milk in its container and I poured that over the coffee, chocolate syrup over that. Really good. The radio was playing really good music. Some singer sang Coltrane's prayer over the top of a different love supreme. Like the Borges story about the guy who rewrote *Don Quixote* word-for-word but the story's different because the writer's different. Borges is Really Good. Like my crazy sailing friend Crowhurst. I put all the fruit on the table into the blender and bent over it while the air came from the bottom of the blender smelling like electricity. And that was really good and better with the carrots in. I walked through the park marveling at how beautiful the dogs and trees and women were. The tracks going from tree to tree in the snow had to be squirrel, and they leave wonderful tracks. Like exclamation points everywhere. Which there are if you look. Really look. An example. In the parking lot of the dollar-movie theatre I saw two young men in heavy metal shirts. They looked dull and fat and stupid. Then, in the open cab of a truck, one of them leant over the other and fastened his seatbelt the way I'd tuck a lover into bed. He made sure his friend, who was just slow, not dull, was safe. And then I started to believe.

Room 9/11: the Case of   the Missing Pilot
—for Michael Richards

The violence of memory   recedes & expands in direct
competition w/ what is imagined — things said yesterday
or this morning disappear before lunch — while the clothes
we wore as children return   again to fashion unimaginably.

Somewhere near the thirty   -second floor, if the floor we
jump from is the ninety -second, having arrived, physically,
at this moment through the stairwell window, our fire-escape,
we get lost in the, um,   concrete aspects of our body—

but what brought us here   has far more to do w/ memory.
W/out memory we are   as senseless animals, no, that's not
right, animals remember,   violence, we are burning bones
w/out memory. W/out   memory there is no reflection,
w/out reflection there is no sorrow—w/out sorrow there is no

joy.

There is no mystery resolved by the body that w/out
memory does not dissolve   into cipher. There is no mystery
the body cannot solve   nor does not solve in time.

Ground floor.

The Sad Affair of Room 19 Concluded: Cold Case Closed

:if we walk into the pawn shop clutching the home stereo
:if we are in a dirty t-shirt that shows a bloody
                               constellation inside our elbow
:if dots down to the vein between our first two knuckles
:if the stars smell like Neosporin
:if we sell the jeep to a drug dealer
:if we don't remember doing that
:if our brother takes a shot-gun out of our hands
:if he tackles our sobbing hulk on the lawn
:if X & her undergrad intern watch from the porch
                               w/ an imaginary bowl of popcorn
:if we miscradle the pay phone when she hangs up on us
:if miscradle is really us smashing the phone's chrome
                               face plate crying
      how much time do we get for how much money?
:if her mother hears about us opening her mail
:if how we infringe the restraining order
:if her family attorney wants jail time
:if we spend more than half an hour at our shitty
                               chainsaw-in-hand job sobbing
:if we're being paid minimum wage for the trees
                               we're not cutting down
:if we have to sell our house to get out of town
:if when we see her next is in this bookstore a decade later
:if when we see her we possess a moment
                               & so rob it of all anticipated hurt
:if then a happiness fills the air she made a hole
                               for when she left
:if when we read this a light starts to shine around us

Efficiencies

1:
One aerosol can of clear-varnish sprayed from ankle height onto runway
One stranger selected at random and followed to their terminal gate
One one-way ticket
One suitcase packed so to confuse security x-rays
One uncomfortable seat
One baby crying
One place to go
On

2:
Two days in the air
Two hands
Two cards selected at random from innumerable decks
Two big people turn into two little people
Two engines of reciprocation: cruel, beautiful
Beginning, end

3.
Every motel is an apostrophe
Speaking to something missing

4.
That dark place where lack of evidence
Is evidence—

Nocturne in D

Were you ever so poor that you wore a dress til it fit?
I knit you a scarf of yarn spun
From the pebbles of fluff pulled
From the tip of my phonograph
Needle and when you put it on
& wear it in the wind   plays

You Did Me A Favor the Day You Left

I didn't realize how naieve I was until well
read — then ah got unnaieve as quick as I

could, got old, lost friends, had kids — now
spend my time trying to ununnaieve me.

You two —

the empty chair, the light on for the unsolved
mystery that's never coming home, an old photo

graph tucked into a book of haystack postcards,
the demand for an unnecessary degree of exactitude

in the diagnosis playing counterpoint to complete
apathy as regards treatment: call this part the beat down

she said am I missing something
& then I said you mean that rhetorically right?

Good Wolf & Bad Wolf Have A Truth-Telling Contest

Good Wolf: I have beauty in my life—
Bad Dog: I have satisfaction

Good Wolf: I understand beauty's beauty because temporary—
Bad Dog: I forget we've met when you leave the room

Good Wolf: what is best honors the pack—
Bad Dog: what is best satisfies me best

Good Wolf: there are two ways to name each thing—
Bad Dog: there is only one true name for each thing: me.

Good Wolf: there is only one true name for each thing: us.

Upon Request Bad Dog Sends a Selfie

Which one hides my crazy best?
My thinning fur?
My chip-&-seal scarred nails?
Is there one in which you can't intuit my police file?
My weeping exes?
My insatiable appetites?
My petty pretty anger?
My ravenous jealousy?
My heruculean entitlement?
My boundless propriety?
My endless monologue?
My me, me, me?

The Black Hole Room

●

Mark Hennessy lives in Lawrence, KS.

www.ingramcontent.com/pod-product-compliance
Lightning Source LLC
Chambersburg PA
CBHW021450080526
44588CB00009B/776